SNAKES THAT SLITHER: FUN FACTS ABOUT SNAKES OF THE WORLD

BABY PROFESSOR

EDUCATION KIDS

Snakes belong to the
animal class reptiles.

Snakes are elongated, limbless, flexible reptiles. Snakes are cold blooded animals. Their body temperatures match that of their surroundings.

Snakes do not have ears. They use
their tongues to detect smells to find
food or stay away from enemies.

Snakes don't have legs. They must use
the action of their scales and muscles
to move their bodies across the ground.

Snakes skin is made of a variety of sizes
of scales. A snake continues to grow
throughout its life. They periodically shed
their skin as part of this growing process.

Snakes are carnivorous. They eat a variety of animals. They eat their prey whole and are able to consume prey three times larger than the diameter of their head.

Venomous snakes have special glands and teeth designed to inject venom into their prey. The young are more dangerous than older snakes, because they're more likely to strike.

There are 700 species of venomous
snakes in the world. Around 250 of
those can kill a human with one bite.